HOW TO GROW ᴀɴ AIR PLANT ꜰᴏʀ BEGINNERS

A Complete Practical Step by Step Guide to everything you need to know about air plants; tips and care instructions for air plant beginners

Mark B. Owens

How to grow an air plant for beginners

© 2023 by Mark B. Owens

Table of Contents

Introduction

In a world where the pace of life seems to quicken with each passing day, a curious soul found solace in the most unexpected of places – a single, delicate plant suspended in air. Imagine a quaint little room with sunlight streaming through a large window, casting a warm embrace upon an arrangement of peculiar plants. But it was the one seemingly weightless inhabitant that captured the heart and imagination of our protagonist.

The air plant, or Tillandsia as it's scientifically known, stood as a testament to nature's ingenuity. It needed no soil to thrive, instead drawing sustenance from the very air we breathe. Its leaves stretched out like the arms of a celestial dancer, adorned with a graceful crown of blooms that seemed to defy gravity itself. Its presence held a certain magic, an invitation to explore the enchanting world of these captivating beings.

Our journey begins here, in the embrace of this tranquil room and the alluring mystery of air plants. As the caretaker of this remarkable specimen, you find yourself drawn into a story of growth, connection, and nurturing. Just as the air plant thrives despite its unconventional lifestyle, so too will you flourish as you learn to cultivate, tend, and celebrate these gentle companions.

Through the pages of this book, we shall unravel the secrets of air plant care – a journey that transcends the ordinary and ventures into the extraordinary. From selecting the perfect tillandsia to creating breathtaking displays that seem to defy logic, you are about to become a steward of the ethereal, a cultivator of tranquillity.

So, open your heart to the wonder of air plants, and let the story unfold. As you turn each page, you'll find the guidance and inspiration you need to embark on a green odyssey, discovering the profound joy of growing and thriving alongside these exquisite creatures.

Chapter 1

Getting to Know Air Plants

What is an air plant

Air plants, scientifically known as Tillandsias, are a fascinating group of epiphytic plants that belong to the Bromeliaceae family. Air plants, in contrast to conventional plants, have developed to survive without having direct touch with soil. These unusual plants are indigenous to a variety of environments in Central and South America, where they frequently grow affixed to trees, rocks, or other objects while absorbing moisture and nutrients from the rain and air. They differ from normal plants in that they can absorb nutrients and water through specialised trichomes on their leaves, which makes them a popular choice for imaginative indoor displays and unusual outdoor arrangements. Air plants are popular among plant lovers and interior decorators because of their wide range of shapes, sizes, and colours.

Air plants require good air circulation, bright, indirect light, and a regular misting or soaking to ensure they get the moisture they require. Although they don't require conventional soil, they can be mounted on driftwood or other supports, placed in attractive containers, or hung in terrariums. Air plants have become popular as adaptable and alluring additions to contemporary interior design and horticulture because to their low maintenance requirements and striking look, bringing a touch of the exotic into homes and venues all around the world.

Different types of air plants

There are many different types and species of air plants (Tillandsias), each with unique traits, hues, and growth patterns. Here are some notable air plant species:

1. Tillandsia ionantha: One of the most well-known air plants, T. ionantha is available in a range of shapes and hues, from green to scarlet. Despite being very small, it blooms for a short time and produces colourful flowers.

2. Tillandsia xerographica: T. xerographica is distinguished by its distinctive look, which includes thick, silver-gray leaves that come together in a rosette. When compared to other air plants, it can grow rather large and has a distinctive, alluring presence.

3. Tillandsia bulbosa: This species is distinctive for having long, curly leaves that frequently mimic sea life or tentacles. It has a colourful inflorescence during its flowering season and can be hung upside down.

4. Tillandsia capitata: T. capitata stands out visually thanks to its dense, bulbous shape and silvery foliage. Its appearance is coloured slightly by a tall, reddish inflorescence that it produces.

5. Tillandsia aeranthos, often known as the "Silver Dollar" air plant, has delicate, silvery leaves that give it a charming, attractive appearance. When in bloom, it produces purple blooms.

6. Tillandsia stricta: This species is distinguished by stiff, erect leaves with occasionally slightly curled tips. It blooms with vibrant tubular flowers and comes in a variety of colours, including green, red, and purple.

7. Tillandsia brachycaulos: This eye-catching air plant has a strong scarlet or deep green colouring. During the flowering stage, it often takes on a rosette shape and releases colourful, tubular blooms.

8. Tillandsia streptophylla, also referred to as the "Shirley Temple" air plant, has unusual, twisted, and deformed leaves

that give it a cartoonish appearance. When it blooms, a tall, pink inflorescence is produced.

These are only a few of the several Tillandsia species that are available, each with unique visual appeal and maintenance needs. There are countless creative display and arrangement options available with air plants, which are highly diverse and make fantastic additions to both indoor and outdoor environments.

Fun facts and unique features

Certainly! Tillandsias, or air plants, have many interesting facts and distinctive characteristics.

1. Epiphytic lifestyle: Air plants are epiphytes, which means they can grow on things like trees or rocks without absorbing their nutrients from them. Through specialised trichomes on their leaves, they draw moisture and nutrients from the air and rain.

2. No Soil Required: Air plants don't require soil to grow, unlike most other plants. They are therefore adaptable for artistic exhibits in diverse contexts.

3. Adaptive Trichomes: Trichomes, which resemble microscopic hairs on air plant leaves, aid in the plant's ability to absorb water and nutrients from the surrounding environment. The distinctive silvery or fuzzy look of air plants is also a result of these trichomes.

4. Bromeliad Family: The Bromeliaceous family, which also comprises intriguing plants like pineapples, includes air plants.

5. Variety of Shapes and Sizes: There are many different types, sizes, and colours of air plants. While some have dense, succulent-like foliage, others have slender, fragile leaves.

6. Flower Variety: Air plants generate a range of vibrant, frequently fragrant blooms when they bloom. The blooms' visual appeal is increased by the fact

that they can emerge in a variety of shapes, from tubular to spherical.

7. Slow Growth: Air plants live longer because of their slow growth. Some species can live for a number of years with adequate care and even produce offsets, or "pups," that can develop into new plants.

8. Flexible Display: Because air plants don't require soil to grow, they can be creatively displayed in glass terrariums, as hanging ornaments, or placed on driftwood or stones.

9. Air plants are sensitive to light and water, and both overwatering and underwatering can harm them. Their health depends on striking the correct balance and recognising their unique requirements.

10. Blooms of Air Plants: Air plants usually only produce blooms once in their lifespan. The mother plant may gradually deteriorate after flowering, although it frequently produces additional offsets before going extinct.

11. Natural Air Purifiers: By collecting pollutants and releasing oxygen during photosynthesis, air plants, like many other plants, can help improve the quality of the air.

12. Habitat Adaptation: To live in their natural environments, air plants have developed a variety of adaptations. While some plants may survive drought and desiccation, others prefer humid conditions.

13. Hybridization: By breeding several species of air plants, plant hobbyists and growers have produced a large number of hybrids. The result has been an increase in the variety of colours, forms, and sizes.

14. Easy to Propagate: Air plants are generally simple to grow from seed. Offsets from the parent plant can be separated and allowed to develop into new independent plants.

15. Global Popularity: Due to their unusual appearance and low maintenance requirements, air plants

are now widely available to a variety of plant enthusiasts.

Air plants are a favourite among plant collectors and enthusiasts thanks to these fascinating traits and facts that add to their attractiveness and charm.

Chapter 2

Selecting Your Air Plants

Choosing healthy plants

When selecting healthy air plants, keep an eye out for lively and colourful foliage and stay away from any wilting or discolouration symptoms. Avoid plants with dry or shrivelled leaves by making sure they have a turgid sensation, which indicates proper hydration. Check the leaves and trichomes for bugs or signs of damage. Choose plants with robust bases that are firmly anchored since this signal strong anchoring and growth. Additionally, choose plants that have offsets or evidence of new growth, as these indicate health and possibility for growth in the future.

Popular species for beginners

Due to their relatively simple maintenance requirements, a number of air plant species are particularly well-suited for beginners. For people who are new to air plant gardening, the following popular species are excellent choices:

1. Tillandsia ionantha: This species is a favourite with novices because it comes in a variety of colours and sizes. It is resilient and accommodating, and because of its modest size, it is perfect for little displays.

2. Tillandsia xerographica: Despite being bigger, T. xerographica requires remarkably little upkeep. Beginners seeking for a distinctive centrepiece will find it to be a fantastic option due to its striking appearance and slow growth pace.

3. Tillandsia stricta: T. stricta is a low-maintenance plant that can survive in a range of environments and has an upright growth habit and colourful inflorescence.

4. Tillandsia capitata: The species Tillandsia capitata is renowned for its unique textures and bulbous appearance. It is beginner-friendly because to its tolerance for different light levels and general durability.

5. Tillandsia brachycaulos: T. brachycaulos is adaptable and can exhibit a variety of colours depending on the amount of light and moisture. It appeals to beginners due of its small size and simple maintenance requirements.

6. Tillandsia bulbosa: This plant is a fascinating and eye-catching option because to its peculiar, curly leaves and capacity to hang upside down. It can survive in a variety of environments and is comparatively forgiving.

7. Tillandsia aeranthos: The "Silver Dollar" air plant has silvery leaves that lends elegance to any arrangement and is little maintenance.

8. Tillandsia harrisii, also referred to as the "Spider Plant," is a plant with a

peculiar, wispy appearance that can grow in a variety of environments.

These species are great for people who are new to caring for air plants because they often have simple maintenance requirements and are more tolerant of minor mistakes. As with any plant, it's critical to learn about and comprehend the particular requirements of the species you select in order to maintain their health and growth.

Sourcing air plants

Finding air plants can be a fun and rewarding process. There are various choices available to you. You can benefit from viewing and choosing healthy plants in person by visiting local plant nurseries and garden centres, which frequently provide a selection of air plants. Online retailers and specialised plant stores provide a broad variety of air plant species, hybrids, and uncommon types if you're seeking for convenience and a vast selection. To make sure the plants are delivered in good condition while making an online purchase, be careful to read reviews, look into the seller's reputation, and find out how the plants will be handled and shipped. Additionally, think about going to local plant markets, plant fairs, or gardening events since these may be fantastic places to find unusual and locally grown air plants and meet other plant lovers.

It's critical to select trusted vendors or suppliers when buying air plants who put the health and welfare of their plants first. Always thoroughly inspect the plants before buying, whether you choose to buy from a local nursery, an internet retailer, or a plant fair. Look for healthy indicators such as lush, solid attachment to the base, absence of damage or pests, and vivid foliage. Make sure the plants are identified by their correct species or variety names, and if you have particular care requirements or objectives, don't be afraid to approach staff members who are educated about plants or other gardeners for advice. Finding air plants can result in a beautiful collection that adds natural beauty and charm to your area if you go about, it the proper way.

Chapter 3

The Essentials of Air Plant Care

Light requirements

Depending on their species and natural environments, air plants require different amounts of light. They typically do best in direct, strong light. The various light levels and how they affect air plants are broken down as follows:

1. Bright Indirect Light: For the majority of air plants, this is the best lighting situation. Put them in a spot where they

get bright, indirect light for the majority of the day, such as close to a window with filtered sunlight. They should not be exposed to intense, direct sunlight since this might cause sunburn and dehydration.

2. Low to Medium Indirect Light: While some air plants, like Tillandsia stricta and Tillandsia bulbosa, can withstand lower light levels, their growth may be more sluggish and their coloration may be less intense. Make sure they continue to get some daylight throughout the day.

3. Bright, Indirect Morning Light: Compared to the afternoon sun, the morning sun is frequently softer and less strong. It may be advantageous to place your air plants in an area that receives bright, indirect morning light.

4. Artificial Light: You can use artificial grow lights made for plants if you're

growing air plants indoors or don't have access to natural light. Choose LED lights with a wide spectrum, and place them 6 to 12 inches above the plants. Ten to twelve hours a day should be spent keeping the lights on.

Keep in mind that because they originate from a variety of habitats, such as woods, deserts, and higher elevations, air plants' preferred lighting conditions can vary. You can change your air plants' placement if necessary by tracking how they respond to the light over time. They can be sensitive to alterations, so take care not to expose them to abrupt variations in light levels. While enough light can cause solar damage, insufficient light can cause sluggish growth and potential health problems. To ensure the general health of your air plant species, you should strike a balance based on their unique requirements.

Watering techniques
(submersion, misting, soaking)

Because of their specific structure and ecological adaption, watering air plants is an essential part of their maintenance. Here are three typical methods for watering air plants:

1. **Submersion**: An effective way to thoroughly hydrate air plants is to submerge them in water. Water should be at room temperature. Gently submerge the air plants in the water. Make sure the entire plant is immersed and let them soak for 20 to 30 minutes. Place the plants upside down on a towel to dry for a few hours after soaking, then put them back in their display. Gently brush off any leftover water.

2. **Misting**: Using a fine mist spray bottle, misting entails misting water over the leaves of air plants. 2-3 times per week, mist the plants to keep the leaves uniformly moist but not soggy. For plants that like greater humidity levels, misting is appropriate, but in

drier conditions, it might not be sufficient to hydrate the plant adequately.

3. **Soaking:** Similar to submersion, soaking entails prolonged immersion. The air plants should soak in water for a minimum of two hours. If the plants have been exposed to very dry conditions, this procedure might be performed on occasion to promote a more thorough hydration.

Take into account the following advice while selecting a watering method:

- Frequency: The frequency of watering is influenced by the humidity, light intensity, and particular type of air plant, among other things. Water your plants, on average, 1-3 times per week, modifying as necessary based on your observations of their requirements.

Use purified or filtered water, or leave tap water out overnight to let the chlorine evaporate. Use softened water sparingly since air plants might be harmed by the salts in it.

-Drying Time: After using any type of irrigation, make sure the plants have enough airflow to prevent rot. To avoid problems, they should dry in 4 hours.

- Temperature: To avoid stunning the plants, use water that is at normal temperature.

- Leaf Bases: After watering, pat the base of the leaves gently to drain any extra water that may have accumulated and could have led to rot.

- Avoid Overwatering: Air plants frequently suffer from overwatering. To avoid root rot, make sure they are completely dry before the next watering.

- Observation: Keep an eye out for overwatering (rotting or mushy base) and underwatering (curling or wrinkling foliage).

In the end, you can give your air plants the best care by being aware of their individual requirements and modifying your watering schedule in response to your surroundings and their reaction.

Humidity needs

Because they evolved in a variety of settings with different humidity levels, air plants (Tillandsias) have different humidity needs. Compared to many other houseplants, air plants often do better in situations with higher humidity, though the particular requirements of each species can change depending on the growing environment. Keeping the plants adequately damp prevents them from drying out and promotes their general health. Your air plants could need less added humidity if you reside in a tropical climate or another area with naturally greater humidity levels. To make sure your air plants have enough moisture, you might need to go above and beyond if you live in a dry region or during the heating season inside.

There are numerous ways you might use to satisfy their humidity requirements. The local humidity can be increased by regularly spraying the plants' leaves with room-temperature water. A more humid microclimate can also be produced by placing the air plants in a humidity tray with water and small stones, making sure the bases of the plants are raised above the water. By placing air plants in a group, the humidity level surrounding them will naturally rise. Maintaining appropriate humidity levels can also be helped by providing excellent air circulation while avoiding very dry areas, such as those near heating vents. Your air plants will stay healthy and alive if you keep an eye on their appearance and modify your humidity-enhancing procedures as necessary.

Temperature considerations

Temperature is an important factor in the care of air plants (Tillandsias) as it can influence their growth, blooming, and overall well-being. While different species have varying temperature tolerances based on their native habitats, there are some general temperature considerations to keep in mind.

Most air plants thrive within a moderate temperature range, typically between 50°F to 90°F (10°C to 32°C). This means they can adapt well to indoor environments and are suitable for various climates. Avoid exposing air plants to extreme temperature fluctuations, as rapid changes can stress the plants and lead to issues like leaf burn or dehydration.

During colder months, be cautious of exposing air plants to freezing temperatures, as frost can severely damage or kill them. If you live in a region with cold winters, consider bringing your air plants indoors or providing them with extra protection during chilly nights. Similarly, excessive heat, especially combined with low humidity, can lead to desiccation and stress. Keep air plants away from direct sunlight and intense heat sources during hot weather.

Regularly monitor your air plants for signs of temperature-related stress, such as browning or drying of leaves. Providing a stable temperature environment and adjusting their placement based on seasonal changes will help ensure your air plants remain healthy and thrive throughout the year.

Chapter4

Creating the Perfect Environment

Designing a suitable display

Light, humidity, temperature, and aesthetics must all be carefully considered when creating the ideal environment for air plants. Creating a proper display is a fun part of caring for air plants since it enables you to highlight their distinct beauty while guaranteeing their wellbeing. You may design a beautiful display and create the perfect habitat for air plants by following these steps:

1. Pick the perfect Place: Place your air plants in a location that offers them with the perfect quantity of bright, indirect light. If necessary, take into account location near a window with filtered sunlight or a space with appropriate artificial lighting. Avoid the sun's direct rays since they can burn the foliage.

2. Increase Humidity: Since air plants prefer moist environments, water the plants frequently, use a humidity tray, or gather them together to increase the microclimate's humidity. Keep air plants away from draughty areas and heating and cooling systems that can cause humidity levels to drop.

3. Keep the Ideal Temperature: To avoid stress, make sure the temperature is kept between 50°F and 90°F (10°C and 32°C). Refrain from subjecting air plants to abrupt temperature changes or freezing temperatures.

4. Pick a Creative Display: opt for a container or arrangement that blends well with the design of your house and your air plants. Glass terrariums, ornamental bowls, hanging pots, driftwood, and mounted displays are among the options. To avoid decay, take into account materials that won't retain a lot of moisture.

5. Adequate Air Circulation: Adequate air circulation ensures that your air plants dry out after watering by preventing stagnant moisture. Avoid placing your exhibit in a small, enclosed room and instead choose a location with good airflow.

6. Mounting and Securing: Use glue, wire, or other appropriate techniques to firmly fasten air plants to their display if you're using a non-soil medium. To protect the plant from harm, make sure the base is properly fastened.

7. Regular upkeep and care: Keep an eye out for health indicators in your air plants, modify your care practises to suit

their requirements, and sometimes turn them to get an even distribution of light.

8. Creative Components: Add ornamental accents to your arrangement, such as decorative stones, sand, shells, or other organic accents that go well with your air plants' aesthetic.

9. Personalise Your Design: Showcase your ingenuity by putting your own sense of fashion into the exhibit. To design a distinctive and eye-catching layout, play around with various air plant combinations, arrangements, and heights.

10. Watering and Maintenance: Use the proper watering methods, such as misting, soaking, or submerging, in accordance with the requirements of your air plants and the display you have chosen. To avoid rot, be sure to properly dry after watering.

You may create a magnificent and caring environment that accentuates your air plants' beauty while fostering their health and longevity by carefully taking into account these factors.

DIY terrariums and containers

A innovative and pleasant approach to display these unusual plants is by making DIY terrariums and containers for air plants. Pick a glass container that complements your aesthetic and the size of your air plants to start. You can use hanging glass globes, vases, bowls, or even jars. Make sure the container has a large enough entrance so the air plants can be easily inserted and removed.

To ensure efficient drainage and avoid water buildup, layer the bottom of the container with aesthetic materials like rocks, pebbles, or sand. For added visual appeal, you can also include tiny decorative stones, shells, or pieces of driftwood. Place your air plants into the container with care, and then use clear adhesive putty, wire, or twine to secure them. Consider the sizes, shapes, and colours of the plants as you arrange them, making sure to give adequate room for airflow. After placing your air plants, you may further customise the terrarium by including minor ornamental elements or even miniature figures if you so choose. Adjust your watering schedule to suit the enclosed habitat and place your DIY terrarium in a spot with strong, indirect light. Rot can be prevented by ensuring thorough drying between waterings. You may make beautiful and distinctive terrariums that incorporate the beauty of air plants into your home decor with a little imagination and attention to detail.

Mounting options (wood, wire, shells, etc

An inventive method to showcase the natural beauty of air plants is by mounting them. For mounting, a variety of materials are available, each with a unique appearance. A common choice is wood, such as driftwood or branches, which has a natural, rustic appearance. Ensure a tight fit while protecting the air plants by securing them to the wood with wire, twine, or non-toxic glue. Wire is a flexible material that offers a clean, contemporary look and the ability to mould and hold air plants in place.

Shells can be utilised as mounts for a coastal or beach-inspired theme. Use thin wire or clear fishing line to attach air plants to shells to create a one-of-a-kind display that combines the elegance of the plant with the allure of the sea. The mounting of air plants onto ornamental stones or pebbles, which can be grouped in patterns or motifs to increase visual interest, is an additional choice. To make one-of-a-kind air plant displays, you can get inventive with additional supplies like metal grids, frames, or even recycled objects like old frames or antique cutlery. Regardless of the mounting method you select, make sure the air plant's base is tightly fastened while still allowing for adequate airflow and drainage to avoid moisture-related problems

Chapter 5

Nurturing Growth and Health

Fertilizing your air plants

In order to provide air plants, the nutrients they require for strong development and vibrant blooms, fertilising is a crucial part of their care. Apply a water-soluble, water-diluted fertiliser made exclusively for epiphytic plants to the leaves as part of the normal watering process. Generally speaking, you can fertilise your air plants every 2-4 weeks, especially during their active growing season (often spring and summer), and you can cut back on or stop fertilising at this time of year when they are resting. Avoid overfertilizing since too much nutrients can cause burning or other problems. Your air plants will benefit from proper fertilisation over the long term by receiving the right amount of light, water, and other care.

Recognizing signs of health and stress

To properly care for and guarantee the wellbeing of air plants, it is crucial to recognise their health and stress indicators. Healthy air plants have vivid colours, firm to the touch leaves, and steady growth. Look for signs of plant vigour, such as fresh growth in the centre or the appearance of offsets (baby plants) around the base. During their flowering time, healthy plants will also produce a variety of vibrant, well-formed flowers.

On the other hand, stressed air plants may display symptoms like browning or yellowing of the leaves, which may point to problems like being submerged in water or receiving too much sunshine. Dehydration may be indicated by wrinkled or curled leaves, whilst soft and mushy leaves may be an indication of overwatering or decay. It may indicate severe rot if the plant's base turns black or becomes slimy. Additionally, if your air plant stops growing or if its leaves start to seem drab and lifeless, it could not be getting the required attention. These indicators of stress may be addressed and prevented with regular observation and rapid action, such as altering watering, light, or humidity conditions, to ensure your air plants stay healthy and vibrant.

Pruning and grooming

Air plant pruning and grooming are crucial procedures that improve their general health, attractiveness, and longevity. Here are some tips for properly pruning and maintaining your air plants:

1. Eliminating Dead or Dying Leaves: Check your air plants frequently for any leaves that have become damaged, dried out, or turned brown. Use a gentle twisting motion to gently peel these dead or dying leaves away from the plant's base. This promotes new growth,

improves air circulation, and stops decay.

2. Trimming Overgrown Leaves: You can trim your air plant's leaves if they have grown too long or lanky in order to preserve a more even appearance. Trim the leaves down to a desirable length using clean, sharp scissors or pruning shears, keeping in mind the plant's natural shape.

3. Pruning Following Bloom: You could observe that the flowering spike on your air plant starts to wither and die after it has completed blooming. To refocus the plant's energy on new growth or offsets, trim the spent blooming spike near its base.

4. Grooming and Arrangement: To make an attractive arrangement, carefully reposition the leaves of your air plants. For a neater appearance, you can gently bend and arrange the leaves. Make sure the leaves have adequate airflow to avoid moisture buildup and subsequent rot.

5. Pup Removal: Air plants frequently develop offsets or "pups" at the base as they get older. You can carefully remove these pups once they have reached a size that is approximately one-third that of the parent plant. Allow the pup to separate from the parent plant by gently twisting or wiggling it, and then give it time to settle in its new environment.

To prevent the plant from being harmed, pruning and grooming should be done carefully. By following these routine maintenance procedures, you can keep your air plants healthy, maintain their best appearance, and promote new development.

Chapter 6

Troubleshooting Common Issues

Dealing with overwatering and underwatering

It's essential to deal with overwatering and underwatering if you want to keep your air plants healthy. Here are the solutions to each problem:

Overwatering:

If your air plants display symptoms of overwatering, such as mushy leaves, a darkened base, or an unpleasant odour, intervene right once. The afflicted plants should be taken out of the display and gently shaken dry. To allow them to completely dry, place them in a location with good ventilation. If the rot is serious, you might need to use clean, sharp scissors to clip away any damaged areas. Before putting the plants back on display as usual, make sure they are completely dry. Change your watering schedule to avoid overwatering in the future and give the plants time to dry out in between waterings.

Underwatering:

If your air plants exhibit underwatering symptoms, such as curled or wrinkled leaves, modify your maintenance schedule. Soak the plants in room-temperature water for 20 to 30 minutes to rehydrate them. After soaking, gently brush out any remaining water, and then let the plants dry on a towel while upside down before putting them back on display. To maintain the right levels of hydration, spray or water regularly.

It's critical to develop a watering schedule that works for your particular climate and the requirements of your air plants in order to avoid future instances of both overwatering and underwatering. Pay attention to how the leaves and trichomes are doing, and change your care procedures as necessary. The secret to ensuring the health of your air plants is to maintain a balance between hydration and drying out.

Combatting pests and diseases

To keep your air plants healthy, you must fight against pests and diseases. Although air plants are typically less prone to pests and diseases than conventional plants, they can still run into problems. Here is how to respond to them:

Pests:

1. Spider mites: These minuscule parasites can damage and discolour foliage. For more severe infestations, think about using neem oil or insecticidal soap after thoroughly

rinsing the damaged plants with a strong stream of water.

2. Mealybugs: Mealybugs might appear on your air plants as white, cottony lumps. With a cotton swab bathed in rubbing alcohol or a solution made of water and dish soap, you can get rid of them.

3. Aphids: Spraying water on your air plants will help to gently remove aphids. Use neem oil or insecticidal soap for larger infestations.

4. Scale insects: Gently scrape them away with a gentle brush soaked in soapy water. Neem oil also has some effectiveness.

Diseases:

1. Rot: Poor air circulation or overwatering can both cause rot. Prior to putting the plants back on display, make sure they have completely dried off and trim any damaged parts with clean, sharp scissors.

2. Fungal Infections: Excess moisture might lead to fungus problems. Enhance airflow and refrain from overwatering. Applying a copper-based fungicide can aid in the management of microbial issues.

Preventive Measures:

1. Isolation: For a few weeks, quarantine new air plants to make sure they don't spread pests to your existing collection.

2. Proper Air Circulation: Make sure there is adequate air movement to prevent moisture buildup and lower the possibility of fungus problems.

3. Hygiene: Keep your instruments clean and steer clear of touching clean plants with dirty ones to prevent cross-contamination.

4. Regular Inspection: Check your air plants frequently for any indications of diseases or pests. Treatment is made simpler with early discovery.

You can keep pests and illnesses from spreading and harming your air plants permanently by taking immediate action against them. Your air plants will remain healthy and pest-free if you follow routine care procedures like appropriate watering, good lighting, and maintaining a clean atmosphere.

Adjusting care routines for different seasons

As your air plants respond to changes in light, temperature, and humidity, it's crucial to adapt your care practises for the many seasons. Here's how to modify your maintenance schedule for every season:

Spring

a) Light: Increase the quantity of direct, strong light your air plants receive as the days grow longer. During this season, they will begin a more active phase of growth.

b) Watering: Your air plants will probably need to be watered more frequently as the light and temperature increase. Keep an eye on their moisture levels and change your watering schedule as necessary.

c) Fertilization: To aid in the plants' growth and possible blossoming, fertilisation should be started or increased in the spring.

Summer:

a) lighting: Continue to provide plenty of direct, strong light. Be mindful of extreme heat, though, and shield your air plants from the glaring noon light.

b) Watering: Your air plants could dry out more quickly in warmer weather. In order to ensure appropriate drying between waterings, increase watering frequency as necessary.

c) Humidity: Maintain the proper humidity levels, especially if you live somewhere arid. Trays with constant misting or humidity can be helpful.

Fall

a) lighting: As the number of daylight hours decreases in the autumn, alter your air plants' lighting levels to give them a little less light. As the weather drops, keep them away from windows that are too cold.

b) Watering: Reduce watering frequency as the temperature drops and give your air plants more time to dry out between waterings. When the weather is cooler, this helps avoid overwatering.

c) Resting period: Autumn is when many air plants go into their resting phase. Avoid using excessive fertiliser and concentrate on keeping the environment stable.

Winter:

a) light: Because the sun is less intense in the winter, provide the most indirect light possible. If there is insufficient natural light, think about using grow lights to augment.

b) Watering: Reduce watering even more in the winter to avoid plants retaining too much moisture in the chilly air. To avoid rot, make sure the plants are well dried between waterings.

c) Temperature: Avoid freezing temperatures around your air plants, especially if you reside in a cold climate. During chilly evenings, bring them inside or provide them insulation.

d) Fertilising: Since many air plants are in a resting phase in the winter, fertilisation should typically be reduced or stopped.

Your air plants will thrive and adapt to the regular cycles of growth and hibernation if you adjust your care practises to the changing seasons. This will ensure their long-term health and vitality.

Chapter 7

Propagation and Reproduction

Natural lifecycle of air plants

The growth, reproduction, and final decline of air plants (Tillandsias) are all influenced by the several stages that make up their natural lifetime. The natural lifetime of air plants can vary depending on the species, habitat, and growing environment; however, the following broad timetables are typical:

1. Stages of germination and seedlings: The life cycle of an air plant begins with the production of seeds during flowering. Wind disperses seeds, which may touch down on suitable surfaces like rocks or trees. A seedling emerges

after germination and begins to grow its first set of leaves.

2. The juvenile growth phase: The air plant keeps developing and putting out new leaves throughout this phase from its main growing point. It concentrates on developing a strong root system and preparing for future growth.

3. Mature Growth and Reproductive Stage: Around its base, the air plant will produce offsets, also called "pups," as it grows older. When the puppies are big enough, they can be detached from the parent plant and become new plants. A flowering spike that will bear the plant's adult flowers, which are frequently fragrant and colourful, may also start to form. In the life cycle of an air plant, flowering is a crucial phase because it initiates reproduction.

4. The blooming and reproduction stage: As the flowering spike develops, it eventually bears colourful blooms. The flowers attract pollinators like insects or birds, or the wind pollinates them. The plant produces seed pods after

pollination that are filled with tiny seeds that can be blown by the wind to new areas.

5. Decline and Senescence: The parent plant's energy may be redistributed after flowering and seed production, and it may then begin to decrease. Depending on the species, the parent plant may gradually wither away while the offsets it created mature into adult plants and eventually bear their own pups and flowers.

You may take the proper care of air plants and foresee changes in their growth patterns by being aware of their natural lifespan. Regular maintenance procedures, including as appropriate lighting, timely offset propagation, and adequate watering, can prolong the life and health of your air plants.

Producing offsets and pups
A remarkable component of air plant development and reproduction is the formation of offsets, usually referred to

as pups. Offsets grow around the base and are baby versions of the parent plant. Here is how offsets are produced by air plants and how to take care of them:

1. A natural process: Offsets are a normal feature of the life cycle of air plants. These pups are produced by the parent plant using energy, and when they develop into full plants, they will reproduce the process. After the air plant reaches a specific level of maturity and has been exposed to favourable conditions, offsets typically appear.

2. Identifying Offsets: At the base of the parent plant, offsets commonly take the form of tiny rosettes. Even while they may start out little and unnoticeable, they will eventually grow and create their own leaves, roots, and blooming spike.

3. Taking Care of Offsets: Offsets can be carefully divided for propagation once they have gotten to a size that is roughly one-third that of the parent plant. To separate the offset from the parent plant, gently twist or wriggle it. Before separating the offset, make sure it has established roots or a root foundation to boost its chances of effective growth.

4. Propagation and Development: The separated offset should be placed in a suitable area, such as one that is well-ventilated and has bright, indirect light. Stay away from bright sunshine and lots of wetness. The offset can be glued or wire mounted, or it can be planted in a suitable container or growing medium. Give the offset the same attention you would give a mature air plant by misting or watering it frequently.

5. The Cycle is Repeated: It will eventually produce its own pups when the separated offset matures, and the cycle is continued. You can use this method to add fresh air plants to your collection and appreciate their beauty without having to buy more specimens.

Offset production is both a normal occurrence and a fascinating chance for air plant aficionados to propagate and take care of new plants. Offsets can survive and carry on the fascinating lifecycle of air plants with the right care and attention.

Reproduction methods and tips

There are many ways for air plants to reproduce, including via generating seeds, flowers, and offsets. Here are some pointers for each of these methods of reproduction:

1. Producing Offsets (Pups):

- Wait for Maturity: After the parent plant has matured for a while, usually a year or more, offsets begin to develop.
- Gentle Distancing: You can carefully separate the offset once it is roughly one-third the size of the parent plant and has grown its own roots or root base. The offset will come off if you gently twist or move it.
- Root Development: Make sure offsets have a root base or developed roots before planting or mounting them. Their chances of experiencing successful growth will be improved.
- Alternate Care: Give mature air plants comparable attention. Maintain the right levels of light, humidity, and watering to ensure the best possible growth.

2. Flowering and Seed Production:

- Blooming Environment: By maintaining the proper humidity, temperature, and light levels, you may promote flowering. Flowering is frequently triggered by a natural season of increasing light (spring/summer).
- Pollination The blossoms on your air plant must be pollinated in order for it to bloom and set seed. This can be accomplished by the wind, insects, or by delicately transferring pollen from one blossom to another by hand.
- Seed Gathering: The seed pods should be left to develop and dry on the plant. Gently extract the seeds from the pods once they are completely dry.
- Planting Seeds: On an appropriate substrate, such as sphagnum moss or a well-draining mixture, sow the seeds of air plants. To keep the substrate moist enough for germination, mist it frequently.

- Patience: It takes persistence and careful consideration to grow air plants from seeds. Significant growth may not be seen for several months.

3. **Division**:

- Carefully removing the individual rosettes from larger air plants that have formed clusters or dense rosettes will allow you to split them into many plants.
- Gentle Separation: Carefully separate the rosettes without tearing the leaves or roots. Try to keep a few roots on each division, if you can.
- Root Development: Before mounting or planting the separated rosettes, give them time to establish their own root systems.

While growing fresh air plants can be rewarding, it also takes careful maintenance to assure their success. Furthermore, not all air plants produce seeds, and the procedure varies depending on the species. Experimenting with various reproduction techniques can give your air plant trip an interesting new dimension and aid in growing your collection.

Chapter 8

Beyond the Basics: Advanced Care Techniques

Experimenting with different environments

Experimenting with different environments for your air plants can be a fun and educational way to discover the optimal conditions that promote their growth and well-being. Here's how to approach this experimentation:

1. Varied Light Conditions: Try placing your air plants in different locations with varying light levels. Some in brighter, indirect light, and others in slightly shadier spots. Observe how each group responds over a few weeks. This experiment will help you identify the light intensity your air plants prefer and guide you in finding the perfect placement for each species.

2. Humidity Variations: Create microclimates with different humidity levels. Group some air plants together and others in more isolated areas. Implement humidity-enhancing techniques like misting or humidity trays for some while keeping others in lower-humidity environments. Monitor how your plants react to these adjustments. This experiment can provide insight into the humidity preferences of different air plant species and guide you in maintaining suitable humidity levels.

3. Temperature Range: Expose your air plants to varying temperature conditions. Some can experience slightly cooler nights, while others can remain in warmer areas. Observe how the different temperature ranges affect their growth, color, and overall health. This experiment can help you understand the temperature preferences of your air plants and guide you in finding the best seasonal care routine.

4. Watering Methods: Experiment with different watering techniques, such as misting, soaking, or submersion. Keep detailed notes on how each method influences your air plants' health, growth, and appearance. This experiment will help you tailor your watering routine to the specific needs of each species and your local climate.

By conducting these experiments and carefully observing the responses of your air plants, you'll gain valuable insights into their individual preferences. Remember to document your findings to create a personalized care guide that ensures the long-term health and beauty of your air plant collection.

Hybridization and crossbreeding

Crossbreeding and hybridization are methods used to produce new air plant kinds with distinctive traits. Here is a summary of various procedures and their effects:

Hybridization:

Through the process of hybridization, two distinct species of air plants are crossed to produce a hybrid plant that combines characteristics from both parents. As a result, air plants may develop distinguishing characteristics like uncommon colours, sizes, forms, or growth patterns. In order to increase the variety of air plants available to enthusiasts and collectors, hybridization is frequently conducted by botanical hobbyists, breeders, and researchers.

Crossbreeding:

Crossbreeding is a particular type of hybridization that includes mating two members of the same species with different genetic make-ups. The goal of this technique is to improve certain desired qualities in the progeny. Crossbreeding, for instance, might be used to develop air plants with bigger flowers, more vivid colours, or better resistance to particular environmental factors.

Implications:

Hybridization and crossbreeding have several implications for air plant enthusiasts and the botanical community:

- Variety: As a result of these processes, a large variety of air plant types are produced, each with its own distinct traits and look.
- Diversity: Hybridization and crossbreeding help to increase the variety within the air plant genus, giving you more options for

colour, size, and maintenance needs.
- Difficulties: A thorough study of the genetics and upkeep requirements of air plants is necessary to produce hybrids and crossbreeds. It takes rigorous selection and breeding methods to produce live, healthy plants because not all hybridizations are successful.
- Commercial Impact: The release of novel and distinctive air plant types may spark consumer interest in the air plant market by luring in enthusiasts, hobbyists, and collectors.
- Conservation: By retaining their genetic features in hybrid offspring, hybridization and crossbreeding can aid in the conservation of uncommon or endangered species.

It's crucial to remember that hybridization and crossbreeding should be done professionally and ethically, taking into account the welfare of the plants and the potential effects on their genetic variety in the long run. While preserving the unique natural traits and preservation of these intriguing plants, these procedures can contribute to the dynamic and always changing world of air plant culture.

Collecting rare and exotic air plant varieties

For collectors who are interested about these unusual plants, collecting rare and exotic air plant types may be a thrilling and gratifying endeavour. In order to harvest uncommon and exotic air plant species, follow these steps and take the following into account:

1. Education and research: Start by learning about the various types and kinds of air plants. Learn about their native environments, upkeep needs, developmental cycles, and distinctive traits. It will be easier for you to give the

plants you're interested in the right care if you have an understanding of them.

2. Reliable Sources: Buy air plants from trustworthy and moral vendors, such as accredited online retailers, botanical gardens, or specialised nurseries. Look for vendors who are honest about the origins, upkeep requirements, and cultivation techniques of the plants.

3. Participate in plant exhibitions and events: A vast variety of air plant kinds, including uncommon and exotic ones, are frequently available at botanical exhibitions, plant fairs, and expos. These gatherings offer the chance to connect with vendors, view the plants up close, and pick the brains of fellow plant lovers.

4. Establishing Contact with Enthusiasts: Through internet forums, social media groups, and neighbourhood gardening clubs, you can get in touch with other air plant collectors and lovers. Through networking, you can discover unusual kinds, exchange

experiences, and perhaps even trade or buy plants.

5. The CITES Regulations: Be knowledgeable about the CITES (Convention on International Trade in Endangered Species of Wild Fauna and Flora)-governed international laws. These laws may preserve some endangered species of air plants, restricting trade or necessitating import/export licences.

6. Maintenance and Propagation: Once you've obtained unusual air plant kinds, concentrate on giving them the particular care they require. Be ready to change your care regimen to suit their particular needs. You can grow your collection by learning how to reproduce these plants from seeds, offsets, or other sources.

7. Documentation: Keep thorough records of all the rare air plants you own, including their names, places of origin, dates of purchase, and any special care requirements. This material can both be helpful for your own

research and for information sharing with other fans.

8. Environmental ethics and conservation: Make sure that your gathering methods support ethical principles and environmental conservation activities. To safeguard wild populations and promote sustainable production methods, avoid taking plants from their natural habitats and be careful where you get your plants.

It takes continual learning and admiration of these amazing plants to collect uncommon and exotic air plant species. You can take pleasure in the beauty and diversity of air plants while aiding in their preservation by treating your collection with consideration, responsibility, and a commitment to their well-being.

Conclusion

As you reach the end of this journey through the world of air plant care, I hope you've discovered the same wonder and serenity that these remarkable plants have brought to my life. From the moment you welcomed your first tillandsia into your home, you embarked on a rewarding adventure filled with growth, learning, and the joy of nurturing life in its simplest and most captivating form.

Remember, the journey doesn't end here. Just as your air plants continue to evolve and flourish, so does your knowledge and connection with these fascinating organisms. Every misting, every beam of sunlight, and every tender touch will strengthen the bond you share with your air plants.

I encourage you to keep exploring. Experiment with creative displays, try new care techniques, and marvel at the extraordinary beauty of nature's resilient wonders. Share your successes, challenges, and discoveries with fellow enthusiasts – a community as diverse and vibrant as the air plants themselves.

If this book has been a source of guidance and inspiration on your air plant journey, I kindly invite you to share your thoughts with others. Your reviews and feedback on Amazon will not only support the growth of this book but also help budding air plant enthusiasts find their own path to nurturing these captivating companions. Your feedback will help others discover the wonders of air plant cultivation and continue to support the growth of this community. Your words could be the encouragement someone needs to embark on their own rewarding journey. Thank you!

Thank you for embarking on this adventure with me. May your days be filled with the tranquillity of verdant foliage, the marvel of delicate blooms, and the fulfilment of fostering life in its most captivating and ethereal form.

With heartfelt gratitude,

Mark B. Owens

Printed in Great Britain
by Amazon

46238701R00046